Jasper th

by Michèle Dufresne
Illustrated by Sterling Lamet

Pioneer Valley Educational Press, Inc.

Here is Jasper.

Jasper is a cat.

Jasper is a fat cat.

3

Jasper likes to sleep.
Jasper likes to eat.

"Wake up, Jasper,"
said Mom.
"Wake up!"

"Wake up, Jasper,"
said Katie.
"Wake up! Wake up!"

"Jasper likes tuna fish,"
said Katie.
"Look, Jasper!
Here is tuna fish!
Wake up!
Look at the tuna fish!"

Jasper is up!
Jasper is eating tuna fish.
Jasper is a fat cat!